POJ 10-2009

D1014766

My Teacher Dances on the Desk

Poetry by Eugene Gagliano

Illustrations by Tatjana Mai-Wyss

PUBLISHED BY
Sleeping Bear Press

This book is dedicated to all the elementary teachers
who inspire and make learning fun.
—Gene

To my special teachers: Bruno, Marianne, and Mark.
—Tatjana

Text Copyright © 2009 Eugene Gagliano
Illustration Copyright © 2009 Tatjana Mai-Wyss

Sleeping Bear Press™

310 North Main Street, Suite 300
Chelsea, MI 48118
www.sleepingbearpress.com

© 2009 Sleeping Bear Press is an imprint of Gale, a part of Cengage Learning.

Printed and bound in Canada.
10 9 8 7 6 5 4 3 2 1

Library of Congress Cataloging-in-Publication Data
Gagliano, Eugene M.
My teacher dances on the desk / written by Eugene Gagliano ; illustrated Tatjana Mai-Wyss. — 1st ed.
p. cm.
Summary: "Humorous poetry related to the activities of elementary classrooms related to themes such
as the first day back at school, going to see the school nurse, and not being picked last"—Provided by
publisher.
ISBN 978-1-58536-446-6
1. School children—Juvenile poetry. 2. Elementary school teachers—Juvenile poetry. 3. Classrooms—
Juvenile poetry. 4. Elementary schools—Juvenile poetry. 5. First day of school—Juvenile poetry.
6. Children's poetry, American. I. Mai-Wyss, Tatjana, 1972-ill. II. Title.
PS3607.A3585M9 2009
811'.6—dc22
  2008040790

Table of Contents

First Day Back at School

My mom said, "You be careful
Your first day back at school.
Do what the teacher tells you
And don't break any rules."

"Be careful out on recess
In your new jeans today.
Don't run, or jump, or climb.
Oh, please do what I say."

But teacher said at recess,
"Go out and have some fun."
So I joined my friends in tag,
and all I did was run.

Mom said listen to the teacher,
In jeans I shouldn't run.
Took them off behind a tree
So I could have some fun.

[7]

Sue Ann and Kim just giggled,
And Lisa closed her eyes.
The teacher nearly fainted
Among the screams and cries.

I made the teacher angry.
Mom nearly lost her head.
Why'd they get so mad at me?
I just did what they said.

Happy Children

Happy is singing your favorite tune,
Or jumping for joy the first day of June,
Or fishing for trout in a bubbly stream,
Or licking the cone of your favorite ice cream.

Happy is bringing a puppy home from the pound,
Or whirling around on a merry-go-round,
Or riding a bike with the wind in your hair,
Or winning first prize at the county fair.

Happy is catching tadpoles in May,
Or flying a kite on a blustery day,
Or squishing your toes deep in the sand,
Or having a butterfly land on your hand.

Happy is a beachball ready to bounce,
Or a fluffy gray kitten ready to pounce,
Happy can be what you want it to be,
Happy can be, just you and me.

It's in My Desk

I've got something you can have for a treat,
Something delicious, nutritious to eat.

Let's look in my desk; I know it is there.
I put it in there with my underwear.

With my underwear and part of a peach.
I know it is there; I just have to reach.

It might be behind this Kleenex and book,
Mixed with these wrappers; I just have to look.

I know I stashed it way down in the back,
Shoved it in deep, far down into the black.

I don't think I've found your goody just yet,
But I do feel something icky and wet.

I'll pull it out and we'll both take a peek.
Look, a big black banana beginning to leak.

Sorry my friend, but my treat has gone bad.
You don't have to eat this; now aren't you glad?

May I Go See the Nurse?

Miss Martin! Miss Martin!
May I please go see the nurse?

My finger hurts, my leg is sore.
I slammed my thumb inside the door.
I think I'm feverish. Can you tell?
I scraped my knee. I tripped and fell.

My head hurts. I've a stomachache.
I have a rash for goodness sake.
My eyes are red. I'm black and blue.
I'm sneezing lots and coughing too.

My throat is sore, can barely talk.
Pulled a muscle, can hardly walk.
I'm tired and not feeling well.
Just look at me, oh can't you tell?

Miss Martin! Miss Martin!
May I please go see the nurse?

Of course you can, my darling child
If you should get much worse.

Teacher Never Calls on Me

"I know! I know! I know!"
I raise my hand and say,
But teacher never calls on me.
It happens every day.

"Ooo! Ooo! Ooo!"
I stretch my hand up high,
But teacher never calls on me.
No matter how I try.

I strain my face and grit my teeth.
I twist and turn and sigh,
But teacher just ignores me.
I often wonder why.

When I don't know the answer,
And hide by being still,
It's my luck she'll call on me.
I know she surely will.

Always Late

The teacher's always mad at me.
I'm usually late for school, you see.
Call it tardy, or call it late.
School tardiness must be my fate.

Today my teacher won't be mad,
And I won't have to feel so bad.
I'll be at school on time today.
Maybe early, but that's okay.

It's going to be a big surprise.
Ms. Brown will see that I am wise.
What's that, Mama? What did you say?
There is no school. It's Saturday!

You Dressed Yourself

I think your shoes are backwards.
Your colored socks don't match.
Your zipper's down; your shoe's untied,
And your jeans could use a patch.

The shirt you're wearing is inside out,
But that's not what it's all about.
You dressed yourself for school today.
That's so grown-up, I have to say.

Don't Know What to Write

I don't know what to write about.
I can't make up my mind.
I chew my pencil, stew and fret,
But good ideas are hard to get.

I don't know what to write about.
My brain is just a blank.
I twist and jerk and bite my nail.
I think this time I'm going to fail.

I don't know what to write about.
Can't think of anything.
Got no ideas and don't know why.
I think I'll just sit here and cry.

Stinky Sneakers

My mother says my sneakers stink.
My brother says so too.
My father says my sneakers stink,
And so does sister Sue.

I don't know why my sneakers stink,
But everyone agrees.
I'll set them by the garbage can.
Will someone take them please?

[15]

I Love Music

I love to go to music,
For music is my dream.
Ring the bells,
Toot the horn,
Slap the tambourine.

I love to go to music,
And clang the brassy gong,
Clap the sticks,
Learn to dance,
Sing a brand-new song.

I love to go to music,
And play the xylophone,
Rub the blocks,
Beat the drum,
Play them all alone.

I love to go to music.
Someday I'll play guitar,
Sing a song,
Write a song,
Be a superstar.

I Can't Sit Still

I can't sit still.
It's driving me crazy.
I can't do my work.
It's not that I'm lazy.
I can't sit still.

I can't sit still.
My feet keep on slapping.
I can't even think.
My fingers keep tapping.
I can't sit still.

Don't Care

Don't care that two and two are four,
Or that I never shut the door.
Don't care that I can't ever spell,
Or that I'm late for recess bell.

Don't care if I can tie my shoe,
Or if my tennis shoes are new.
Don't care if my hair is out of place,
Or who was first in outer space.

Don't care unless it's time to eat,
Or someone's sitting in my seat.
Don't care unless it's time to go,
Or it's my turn for share and show.

Don't care unless I'm in big trouble,
Or someone tries to burst my bubble.
Don't care unless it's time to play,
Or someone big gets in my way.

The Whoopee Cushion

Bradley put a Whoopee cushion on the teacher's chair.
Sarah said he wouldn't, so I guess it was a dare.

The teacher's old and kind of frail; it wasn't very fair.
I thought he'd get in trouble, but Bradley didn't care.

She didn't seem to notice as she sat down in the chair.
She only smiled, excused herself, and gently fanned the air.

Twirling

Twirling, twirling, twirling,
I watch the sky go 'round.
Whirling, twirling, swirling,
I'm falling to the ground.

Whirling, twirling, swirling,
I swing my arms out wide.
The heavens spin around me.
I watch the clouds collide.

Twirling, twirling, twirling,
I watch the sky go 'round,
Pretend to be a falling star
And tumble to the ground.

Try Again

You can do it. I know you can,
You can do it, so try again.

It's not easy, but you must try.
Give it your best, I'll tell you why.

To be on top of all the rest,
You have to work, and do your best.

Be a winner and play it smart.
Give it your best right from the start.

Attack the task with lots of zest,
Be determined to pass the test.

Be persistent, keep on trying.
Don't be afraid, no more crying.

You can do it. I know you can.
You can do it, so try again.

Will She Notice?

Will she notice? Does she care?
Will she notice my new hair?

Will she notice? Do I dare.
Take off my hat and show my hair?

Will she notice? Should I look?
Should I hide behind a book?

Will she notice? Like the style?
Say it's really cute and smile?

Will she notice? Laugh at me,
Or just pretend she doesn't see?

Oh! She noticed. See her stare.
"What? You really like my hair?"

Winter Recess

The recess bell rang; it was time to go.
Time to go out and jump in the snow.
Time to get ready to go out and play.
My very favorite time of the day.

Took off my shoes and put on my hat.
Put on my snowpants, that made me look fat.
I zipped up my coat, pulled it up tight.
Made sure my scarf and boots were on right.

I was finally dressed and ready to go
Bundled, excited to play in the snow.
"Recess is over!" I heard someone shout.
"It can't be," I said; "I haven't been out."

You and Me

I'm not good with numbers,
Not half as good as you,
But I love to play with words,
I do; it's really true.

We both use pen and paper
To do what we do best.
And each enjoys the other,
Who cares about the rest?

I'm not good with numbers,
As you can plainly see,
But during this old math test,
I wish I wasn't me.

The New Kid

I'm the new kid in class.
And everybody's staring.
Hope they don't make fun of me
Or the new clothes that I'm wearing.

I miss my school and my best friend,
My house and drives downtown.
I miss my friends and my backyard.
I miss my old hometown.

I wish that I could run away.
'Cause I'm feeling pretty sad.
But once I make some new friends
My life won't be so bad.

The Snake

Tommy put a snake in the teacher's desk drawer,
When she opened it, she fell to the floor.
She fell to the floor with a deafening scream,
I'm sure she knew it wasn't a dream.

The snake wiggled and jiggled down to the floor
Then scurried and slithered out the side door.
The teacher jumped up on her desk and said,
"For a moment or so I thought I was dead."

Then she looked at the class as if to say
"Who in this room wished to scare me today?"
Then Tommy admitted, it was he who had tried,
And covered his face and broke down and cried.

The teacher could see that Tommy was sad,
For frightening her and being so bad.
So she scolded him, then gave him a wink
"At least it didn't go down in the sink."

Off the Floor

Jessie ate a spotted bug,
Picked it up right off the rug.
His momma screamed and baby cried.
His older brother only sighed.

Momma called the doctor quick,
Thought that Jessie might get sick.
The doctor said to take a pill,
Before the bug could make him ill.

Jessie seemed to be all right,
But Momma couldn't sleep that night.
His momma warned him, "Please no more!
You shouldn't eat things off the floor."

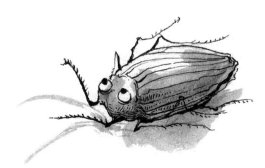

School is Out

School is out! School is out!
Makes me want to sing and shout.
No more classes, summertime,
Games to play and trees to climb.

Camping out and riding bikes,
I'll be taking daylong hikes.
Sleeping late, hide-and-seek,
I'll be having fun all week.

School is out! School is out!
There's no need for me to pout.
My vacation time is here!
No more school until next year.

Show and Share

On Jacob's day for show and share,
He brought his untrained pet.
The children patted the wiggly pup,
And then the puppy wet.

Then Sarah had her turn to share,
She brought a long-haired cat.
When gentle kitty spied the pup,
That was the end of that.

The kitty chased the lanky pup
Right under the teacher's chair.
It scratched the pup and teacher's leg,
And that ended show and share.

Mom Says

Sometimes Mom says I'm wound up,
Or that I am all ears,
Or that it's raining cats and dogs
Which brings me close to tears.

She says to hold my horses,
I've won it by a nose,
And that her promised lips are sealed
And that's the way it goes.

I'll have to put my foot down.
I just might spill the beans.
Cause Mom says face the music.
Do you know what she means?

Move Me Soon

I don't like sitting next to Rose.
She's always picking at her nose,
And chews her fingernails way down,
And always wears a pouty frown.

She slumps and totters in her chair,
And twists and twirls her stringy hair.
Sometimes she slips and passes gas
And grosses all the kids in class.

I don't like sitting next to Rose.
She's always playing with her toes.
Please Ms. Johnson, move me soon.
I don't think I can wait 'til June.

Miss Pringle

Shawna brought her cat to school.
It made Miss Pringle sneeze.
Her eyes began to water,
Then she began to wheeze.

Teacher couldn't catch her breath.
She started to turn blue,
Held her hand upon her chest:
No lie, it's really true.

Shawna brought her cat back home.
Cat's visit was quite brief.
Teacher caught her breath again.
Now that was a relief.

Let Me Be Your Friend

I'll be your friend.
Let me be your friend.
Please, please, please, let me be your friend.

We can teeter-totter,
Swing up to the sky,
Twirl a rope,
Throw a ball,
Laugh until we cry.

I'll be your friend.
Let me be your friend.
Please, please, please, let me be your friend.

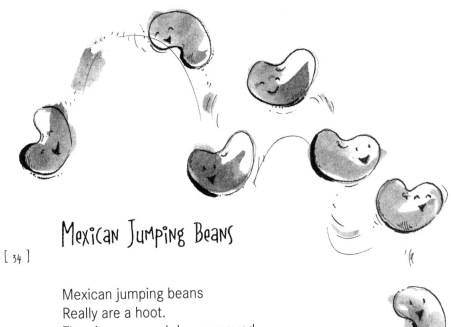

Mexican Jumping Beans

Mexican jumping beans
Really are a hoot.
They jump up and dance around,
But never make you toot.

I Tried to Help the Teacher

I tried to help. I really did.
But I messed up. I'm just a kid.

I overfed the fish; they died.
"Twenty fish!" the teacher cried.

I said, "I'll get the door for you."
And then I stepped upon her shoe.

Shut the door, and slammed her thumb.
She must think I'm awfully dumb.

I dumped the vase on teacher's desk.
Soaked her papers and made a mess.

I tried to help. I really did.
That's what happens when you're a kid.

I Won't Sneeze

Oh no, I think I'm going to sneeze,
But I don't want to, if you please.
There must be something in the air.
It could come from anywhere.

Maybe it's perfume in the breeze,
That always seems to make me sneeze,
Dust or pollen, could be mold,
Or maybe I'm just catching cold.

I'll hold my breath and pinch my nose,
I'll keep that sneeze down in my toes.
'Cause if I sneeze in class, it's true.
I just might sneeze all over you.

I'm Afraid

I'm afraid to open my locker.
I'm scared; I really am.
It could be very dangerous,
Like breaking out a dam.

I'm afraid to open it.
It might crash down on me,
And shove me across the hall,
Like waves upon the sea.

I'm afraid to open it.
I know that it's my fault.
I'm the one who stuffed it,
Like gold inside a vault.

I'm afraid to open it,
And if you're wondering why,
It's full of Halloween candy.
I cannot tell a lie.

[37]

Bobby Benton's Boa Constrictor

Bobby had a snake named Bill.
He kept it on the windowsill,
Until the day it ran away,
Just wanting to get out and play.

Bobby Benton's pet constrictor
Tried to get his little sister,
Chased his mother, chased his father
Tried to get his older brother.

Bobby's boa scanned the floor,
And slithered out the kitchen door.
The lonely snake went off to wander,
Left the house to travel yonder.

Bobby's neighbor Mrs. Fister,
Knew the snake could not resist her.
So she waited until after
Bobby's boa slithered past her.

The slender snake went off to school,
Slid right past the swimming pool.
Slipped between the schoolyard gate,
In such a hurry, it couldn't wait.

Bobby's boa chased a teacher,
Wiggled up and tried to reach her.
All the children made a clatter,
As the class ran pitter-patter.

Out the classroom, past the nurse,
Past a lady who dropped her purse,
Grabbed her toddler from the floor,
And then ran screaming out the door.

Bobby's boa entered the gym,
Climbed the ropes and looked for him,
But his friend Bob was not around,
And so he left without a sound.

Then Bill wriggled toward Miss Pears,
Who went atumbling down the stairs.
The principal just came apart,
Fell into the arms of Mrs. Hart.

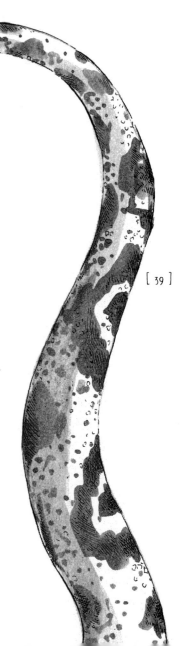

Students screamed and teachers cried.
The secretary nearly died.
But then Bill heard a familiar call,
A friendly voice, from down the hall.

It came from somewhere past the gym,
His friend Bob ran up to him.
I thought I left you on the sill,
You must be lost, my poor friend Bill.

Then Bill curled up on Bobby's arm,
He hadn't meant him any harm.
Bill just missed his closest friend,
And so this story's at an end.

Don't Pick Me Last

I know the game.
You know my name.
I'm super fast.
Don't pick me last.

Don't pass me by.
Please let me try.
I'm very fast.
Don't pick me last.

I'll hit that ball.
I'm not so small.
I'm really fast.
Don't pick me last.

I'm lots of fun,
And I can run.
I'm really fast.
Don't pick me last.

Can't Help It

I don't think I can stand it!
I have to get it out.
I've considered everything.
I have to get it out.

My friends will probably giggle,
My teacher, heave a sigh.
But there's no way to stop it.
I'll have to let it fly.

I hope my friends don't notice,
But if they do I'll yell,
Pinch my nose and wave my hand
And ask, "Who made that smell?"

Caught a Cold

I'm just eight years old,
And I've got a cold.
My nose is stuffy.
My eyes are puffy.
My head feels sleepy.
My eyes are weepy.
Can't breathe through my nose.
Feel bad to my toes.

I'm not feeling well.
Can't wait for the bell.
I must get to bed,
And unplug my head.
I just need some rest.
I know that it's best.
I'm just eight years old,
And I've got a cold.

Fun in the Snow

Children it's time to go out and play,
A chance to play in the snow today.

Be sure not to lie or roll in the snow.
Stay out of the wind when it starts to blow.

Refrain from sliding or gliding on ice,
And don't push or shove, it's not very nice.

Stay off of the monkey and parallel bars,
And please no throwing snowballs at cars.

Children it's time to go out and play,
Go and have fun in the snow today.

Billy Buford's Bubblegum

Billy Buford's troublesome.
He's given me some bubblegum.
Now I'm feeling very glum.
I shouldn't have this bubblegum.

Billy Buford's troublesome,
Gave all his friends some bubblegum.
Now everyone's in trouble some,
Cause teacher said no bubblegum.

Billy Buford's troublesome.
He blew a bubble on his thumb.
Popped it like a kettle drum,
Then Mary Ellen sat in some.

Billy Buford's troublesome,
He gave the teacher bubblegum.
Principal caught her chewing some.
Now teacher's feeling really dumb.

Your Books Are Due

Ms. Shadbolt says my books are due.
My sister says that's nothing new.
I tell my mom the time just flew,
But Mom repeats, "Your books are due."

"Your books are due," my daddy said.
"Look on your desk and under the bed.
They must be returned some time today,
Or you'll get fined and have to pay."

I cannot find them, Mom and Dad.
Please help me look, and don't be mad.
My older brother laughed at me.
He said, "You'll pay a hefty fee."

I searched the bathroom, checked the hall,
But they weren't anywhere at all.
I finally found them on a shelf.
I found the books all by myself.

My Teacher Dances on the Desk

My teacher dances on the desk,
Which may seem kind of strange.
Mom and Dad think he's weird,
But I hope he doesn't change.

My teacher fills his cheeks with air
And twists and turns his face.
Sometimes he makes the grossest sounds.
No one could take his place.

My teacher sprays me on the neck,
And pretends that he just sneezed.
He always makes me feel so good.
I know when he is pleased.

My teacher likes to sing and dance,
Pretends that he can fly.
He always smiles and waves to me
Whenever I pass by.

My teacher snarls and growls at times,
Pretends that he's a cat,
But I know that he cares for me.
I'm grateful just for that.

My teacher dances on the desk
Which may seem kind of strange.
But just between the two of us,
I hope he doesn't change.

Eugene M. Gagliano is known by many children as "the teacher who dances on his desk." Gene is a retired elementary teacher whose author presentations are entertaining, informative, and inspirational. The recipient of the International Reading Association's 2004 Wyoming State Literacy Award, he is also the author of *C is for Cowboy: A Wyoming Alphabet*; *Four Wheels West: A Wyoming Number Book* (2006-2007 Western Writer's Spur Award nominee); *Inside the Clown*; *Falling Stars*; and *Secret of the Black Widow* (2005-2006 Wyoming Indian Paintbrush Award nominee). Gene is also the author of an adult poetry book, *Prairie Parcels*.

Tatjana Mai-Wyss was born in Switzerland. Growing up with her nose in a book, she always wanted to be the one to draw the pictures. Today Tatjana lives in sunny South Carolina where she can work on her screen porch year-round and listen to the birds. Most often she uses watercolor and gouache, adding detail and texture with collage and colored pencils. Her black and white work is usually done the old-fashioned way, in India ink with a dip pen. Find out more about Tatjana at http://tatjanawyss.blogspot.com.